S0-BRP-181

09/24
STRAND PRICE
$ 5.00

to Ellen
You are a Star!
love Kymytstar
xo

Star Von Bunny

HarperEntertainment
An Imprint of HarperCollins*Publishers*

Star Von Bunny

a model tale

STAR VON BUNNY. Copyright © 2007 by House of Fluff, Inc. All rights reserved. Printed in China. No part of this book may be used or reproduced in any manner whatsoever without written permission except in the case of brief quotations embodied in critical articles and reviews. For information address HarperCollins Publishers, 10 East 53rd Street, New York, NY 10022.

HarperCollins books may be purchased for educational, business, or sales promotional use. For information please write: Special Markets Department, HarperCollins Publishers, 10 East 53rd Street, New York, NY 10022.

FIRST EDITION

Book design by Laura Stein
Photographs by Kym Canter and Ruven Afanador

Library of Congress Cataloging-in-Publication Data has been applied for.

ISBN: 978-0-06-134997-3
ISBN-10: 0-06-134997-6

07 08 09 10 11 ID/SCP 10 9 8 7 6 5 4 3 2 1

Everyone is a Star

A portion of the profits from the sale of this book will benefit Doctors Without Borders/Médecins Sans Frontières, an international humanitarian organization providing medical assistance to populations in distress, to victims of natural or man-made disasters, and victims of armed conflict, without discrimination and irrespective of race, religion, creed, or political affiliation.

Six years ago I was
sitting in a suburban bedroom, dreaming of becoming a top model. I was told that it couldn't be done, that it was a long shot, that I wasn't tall enough, pretty enough, or thin enough. I didn't listen to any af it. True, I may not be a conventional beauty, but I've always known I had what it takes to be a star. Some call it an ego; I like to call it a strong sense of self. It took a lot of determination (and a little bit of credit-card debt), but finally all of my dreams are coming true. This is my tale.

The first and most important step to becoming a model is to find a great agent. I start my quest as soon as I arrive in New York City (even in a taxi I'm not one to take a backseat).

There are a few essentials a girl must have before stepping out in a new city.

1. The right designer accessories.
2. A good backstory.

MY BACKSTORY— AKA STAR'S TOP TEN WHITE LIES

Of course, like any good backstory, mine has a few half-truths.

1. I am nineteen years old.

2. I come from the famous Von Bunny clan.

3. I can eat anything I want and never gain weight.

4. I always have at least one fabulous boyfriend in tow . . . and many others waiting in the wings.

5. I never shop, but I always have great clothes.

6. I don't want to be an actress.

7. I am a perfect size 2.

8. I am an intellectual.

9. I couldn't care less about celebrity.

10. I never look at the tabloids.

After

checking out the competition, I start to realize I have something the other girls don't: floppy ears, furry paws. I decide to sign with Bored Model Management. They understand my unique type of beauty.

Bored tells me that the first thing I need to do is make my composite card. This is a model's calling card and is used to introduce me to all of their clients.

Even though I'm perfect, my new agent has a few small suggestions. The first one is that I become a "mono" name. So I quickly banish the "Von Bunny" and join my favorite icons: Iman, Twiggy, Verushka, Cher, Sade, and Madonna.

Steven Mozzarella

STAR

BORED
model management
850 West 13th St.
NY, NY 10013

My agent has a second request: Lose a half inch around my middle. *Everyone* knows the camera adds five ounces. Luckily, losing weight has never been a problem for me. I have always had pretty strict eating habits. I only eat white food. I m convinced you are what you eat.

Patrick Demarshmellowier

STAR

HEIGHT: 18 INCHES
BUST: 14 INCHES
WAIST: 14.5 INCHES
HIPS: 13 INCHES
SHOES: 3
HAIR: white
EYES: brown

Fig Newton

BORED
model management
850 West 13th St.
NY, NY 10013

HEIGHT   18"
BUST   14"
WAIST   14.5"
HIPS   13"
SHOES   3
HAIR   WHITE
EYES   BROWN

FRONT

STAR VON BUNNY

18"

BACK

STAR'S WHITE FOOD DIET

Breakfast

I usually head straight to Starbucks for a grande vanilla crème whip (340 calories).

STAR DIET TIP 1: Having a drink without coffee saves 5 calories.

Midmorning Snack

STAR DIET TIP 2: Breakfast and the midmorning snack can be avoided by sleeping late and going directly to lunch.

Lunch

I stop in any McDonald's and grab a vanilla cone (150 calories).

STAR DIET TIP 3: Ordering the McDonald's vanilla cone instead of the vanilla triple shake (440 calories) will save you enough calories for a midnight snack . . . or another vanilla cone.

Midafternoon Snack

I always carry something with me that does not require a utensil. My favorites are

a can of Reddi-wip whipped light cream (only 15 calories a tablespoon)
marshmallows (only 23 calories per marshmallow)

STAR DIET TIP 4: Never measure out your whipped cream or your marshmallows.

Dinner

At dinner, I exercise my culinary talent and prepare the following:

a skinless baked potato

And I add one of the following "free foods" (aka condiments):

sour cream   butter   ranch dressing

In addition to a strict diet, it is important to have an exercise regimen. I decide to take up yoga.

Since I haven't yet started to work as a professional model, my agent suggests I do a series of test shots to convey my range.

Silly,
Sensual,
Slutty,
Soft, Sad,
and Sexy.

Unless

they have a trust fund (I don't), most aspiring models have to secure odd jobs to supplement their income. I decide that being an artist's model is an easy way to pay the rent until my real modeling career takes off.

Huckscarry for Richard Scarry 2006

In my free time I scour the fashion magazines with my model friends.

TIPS FROM MY MODEL FRIENDS

1. A model should know her face and understand her best and worst features. They tell me I have what is considered to be a round face. As if that's a bad thing? When I look in the camera, it is best for me to be slightly three-quarters in profile and keep my chin low. This will supposedly make my (still perfect) face appear slimmer and more oval.

2. The girls also think my height may be an issue. Yes, I am a little shorter than most models, but they said that to Kate Moss and look at her now. To compensate, they tell me, I need to stand tall with my stomach in and my ears straight. When I do this, I appear to be almost half an inch taller than I really am.

3. Turn your minuses into pluses. I am the only model with a tail. How special is that?

After all my hard work, I finally go out to see and be seen.

I wear
my best
custom-
made
little black
dress for
my French
Vogue
go-see.

Finally
my agent phones to tell me I have my first booking for a top fashion magazine. Of course, I am a little disappointed when I show up and find out that I am not the only model on the set.

**DOUBLE YOUR
PLEASURE:** WEAR A
SKIRT OVER JEANS.
COTTON CORSET,
$825, WRAP SKIRT,
$695, DENIM OVER-
ALLS, NECKLACES, ALL
JEAN PAUL GAULTIER.
BEADED BRACELETS,
ANICE ROSARIO FOR
COMMON GROUND

STAR VON BUNNY'S BACKSTAGE GUIDE, OR HOW TO KISS AND KISS UP, MODEL STYLE

1. Unfortunately, no one wants to watch the model chow down on the catered breakfast (I've learned). You can tell a lot about the client by the food they serve. Big advertising clients have a full spread of hot and cold goodies, but at indie magazines you will be lucky to get a croissant from the local deli.

2. Immediately double-kiss everyone you see. (That's the Euro style, not to be confused with the Colombian one-cheek or the Belgian, Dutch, and Swiss triple-kiss.)

3. Start kissing up to the hairdresser and the makeup artist, since they are responsible for making you look beautiful on the shoot.

4. Kiss up to the fashion stylist as well. She or he is responsible for all the designer clothing and for creating fabulous new looks. If you want to lay it on really thick, compliment their clothes, hairstyle, etc.—they may even give you a piece of clothing from the shoot as a gift.

5. Greet the photographer in a flirtatious yet polite manner. (It is not necessary to pose nude just because he asks you to.)

6. Talk endlessly on your cell phone to your boyfriend. If you don't have a boyfriend, call 777-FILM and whisper sweet nothings to them instead.

7. Ask your booker (this is slang for your agent) to call you often throughout the day. This will make the clients think you are a model in big demand!

8. At the end of the shoot and before you leave for the day, be sure to repeat numbers 2 through 5.

After all that posing (such hard work!), my agent suggests I jet off to Europe to go on casting calls for the fashion show season.

During the breaks in my rigorous schedule *(très difficile)*, I try to soak up *un petit peu de* French culture.

I have always thought of myself as more of an editorial model than a runway model. The endless casting calls begin to confirm this.

BRIONI

CASTING

1° Floor

When I go on my casting call at Chanel, they seem interested in using me as a pincushion instead of a model.

Ouch.

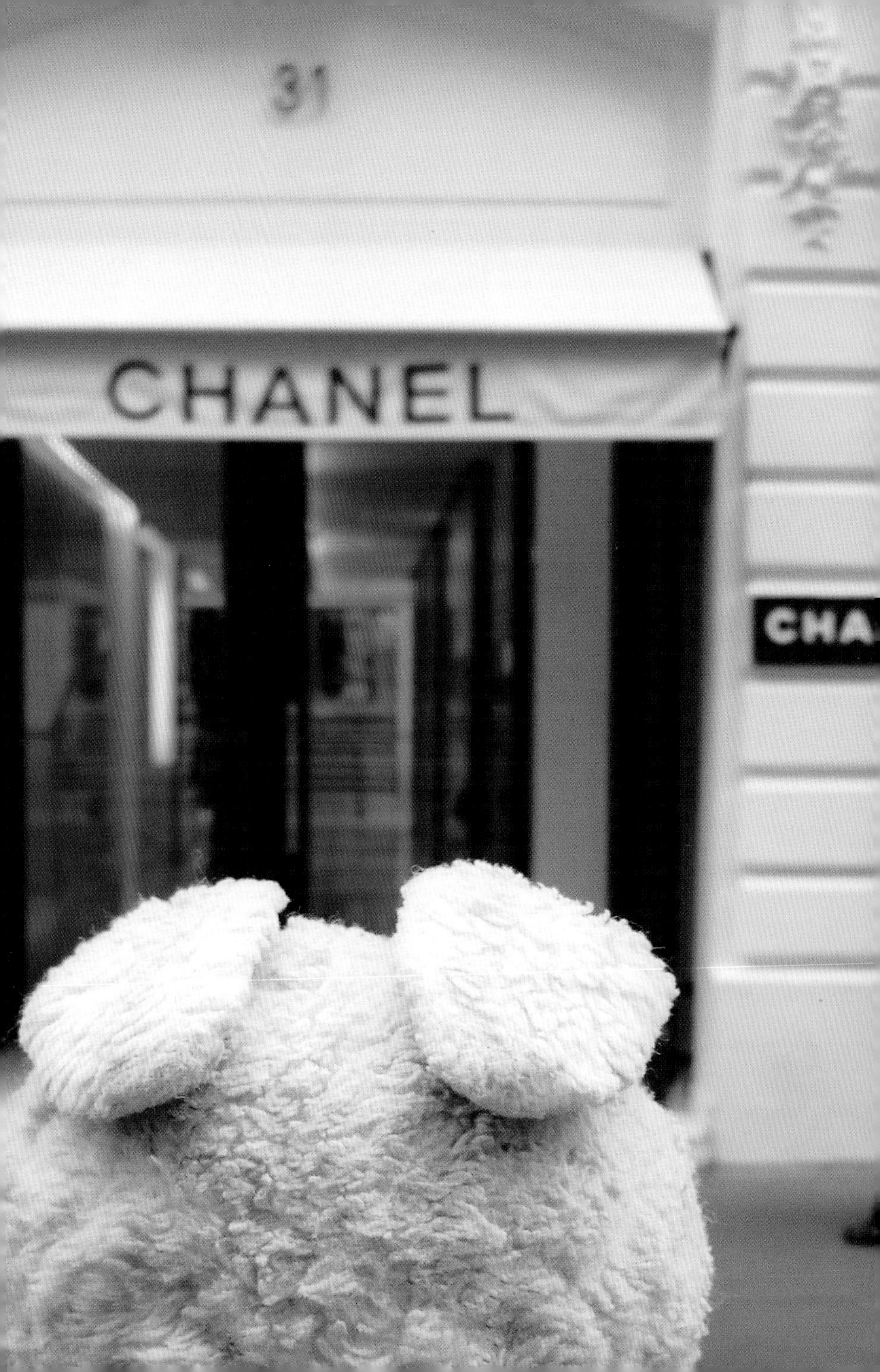
31
CHANEL
CHA

I find retail therapy to be an excellent way of handling rejection.

As everyone knows, just being a model isn't enough these days, so after the European season comes to a close, I head to Los Angeles, the sacred land of the M.A.W.— Model/Actress/Whatever.

10 QUICK STEPS TO BECOMING A M.A.W.

1. Believe in yourself even if everyone else is blind to your potential.

2. Study hard. Read the following classic works:
   Star by Pamela Anderson
   The Truth About Diamonds by Nicole Richie
   House of Hilton by Jerry Oppenheimer
   Everything About Me Is Fake . . . and I'm Perfect
      by Janice Dickinson

3. Always alert the media to your plans, even if it's just a trip to Starbucks.

4. Do at least a small stint in rehab (everyone is addicted to something—my demon is powdered sugar).

5. Find an industry-appropriate boyfriend . . . and then break up with him—dramatically.

6. After you dump said industry-appropriate boyfriend, adopt a child on your own (preferably from a third-world country).

7. Start your own clothing line.

8. Take up a religion (frequently a great stepping-stone to success!).

9. Always Polaroid your outfits before appearing on the red carpet. Visible panty lines and repeating the same look are really big no-no's.

10. Write a book about your life.

After landing in L.A., I immediately go in search of my idol.

Luckily,
a little magazine job materializes.

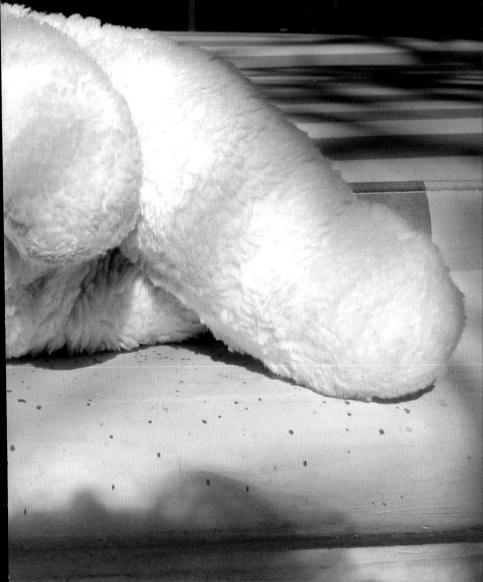

Sadly, it didn't pay enough to cover the bills, but I'd decided long ago that there were certain jobs I would never take.

Pole bunny

As every aspiring M.A.W. quickly learns, there are two L.A.s, the one that you enjoy when you have a job and the one that you put up with while you wait for your agent to call.

THE "I GOT THE JOB" GUIDE TO L.A.

Where to stay:

The Beverly Hills Hotel or the Chateau Marmont. (I am a bit old school when it comes to my hotel choices.)

Where to eat:

For dinner it's Matsuhisa or Mr. Chow. Sometimes I go to the Ivy (it's still good although not that exclusive).

Where to shop:

There are no places better to burn the plastic than Maxfield or Fred Segal.

For vintage, head to Decades. (This is the first stop for young actresses looking for red-carpet dresses.)

Pick up unusual gifts at Skeletons in the Closet, the gift shop at the L.A. County morgue. I mean, who doesn't want a towel with the chalk outline of a body.

Hit up Hyde on Saturday night (though this could be passé by the time this book comes out).

Be sure to use the private paparazzi-free back-door entrance.

THE "WAITING BY THE PHONE FOR MY AGENT TO CALL" GUIDE TO L.A.

Where to stay:

I tolerate the Hollywood Celebrity Hotel—supposedly Marilyn Monroe lived here, though I am sure it was better back then. Or try the Farmer's Daughter Hotel. It's a stone's throw from the CBS studios.

Where to eat:

I love the egg-white omelets at Madame Matisse in Silver Lake, the indie arty neighborhood in Hollywood. (Slumming in Silver Lake is very respectable.)

For fast food, nothing beats Pink's for dogs or In-N-Out for burgers. (Even models who only eat white food make an exception for these joints.)

When you are up in the middle of the night having an anxiety attack because there is still no call, head to Canter's Deli (it's open 24/7).

For a strong cup of coffee and the chance to meet an up-and-coming screenwriter, try the Kings Road Café.

Where to shop:

Wander around the Rose Bowl Flea Market.

While I am waiting to book the next job, I attend acting classes to hone my craft.

I slip past the velvet ropes...

...and then rest by the pool.

I have learned there are all sorts of places in L.A. that provide opportunities to network. It seems that my (equal opportunity) praying is paying off. My agency calls to say that they know someone who knows someone who knows someone's sister who can get me into the Academy Awards. I immediately shift into high gear.

It's crunch time.

The Beverly Hills Hotel
and Bungalows

To: J. Mendel press department
From: SVB
Re: Oscar dress

I have decided to write to you directly instead of using a stylist, because after all I have been dressing myself for the past nineteen years. I believe for something as special as the Oscars only J. Mendel will do. For my very first trip down the red carpet I would like to request one of the following styles from your fall '07 collection. Of course it would be great to have Gilles Mendel's input, as he is one of my favorite *créateurs*!

Look 20—that touch of metallic near my face and trademark ears would be devastating.

Look 25—divine, especially for a girl with a tail.

Look 38—strapless has always flattered my fluffy shoulders.

Let me know what Gilles thinks is best. I believe you already have my measurements on file.

All my love,

SVB

XXXXOOOO

The hair is almost as important as the dress.

I run into my fairy godmother at a pre-Oscar party. She says she has found me the perfect red-carpet date (thirty-four, never married, once had his own TV show). I think, Why not? It worked for that other material girl. I agree to meet him for dinner, but he really isn't my type.

He is much shorter in person . . .

. . . and I refuse to date anyone under two feet. A girl's got to have standards.

I decide to fly solo and immediately begin to work on my Oscar speech, since I'm sure I'll be nominated for something really soon.

Star's Oscar Speech

Oh my god!

Oh my god! I'm sorry this microphone is so much bigger than I am. Um, okay, I would like to thank the Academy (though I am not sure what the Academy is . . .). Mostly I would like to thank myself. I mean, I'm just a girl plucked from a high shelf in a Richard's Hallmark store with a dream. And I can't deny the fact that I like me—I really, really like me! And I am so in love with myself right now. I would, however, also like to thank all the people who helped me get here. First, my model friends, Angela Lindvall, Daria Werbowy, and Gemma Ward for their support and friendship! Christy Turlington for teaching me that beauty is more than skin deep. Thanks to Richard Scarry for employing me when no one else would. To Jean Paul Gaultier, Carine Roitfeld, and Gilles Mendel for being open to my alternative beauty. To my support team, Team Star—Gunnar Petersen and Jonathan. To Trudie Styler for teaching me the importance of love, and lastly but certainly not leastly to Mary-Louise Parker, Bono, Beyoncé, Robert Downey Jr., Derek Jeter, Rosario Dawson, Jennifer Love Hewitt, and Dita Von Teese for helping me to become what I am today.

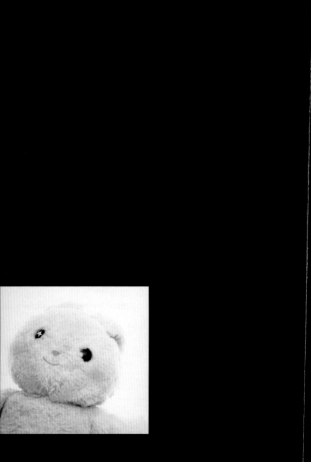

Remember:
Think like a star,
act like a star,
eat like a star,
dress like a star,
and someday
soon you too can
be just like Star!!!

Acknowledgments

Marissa Matteo
Lynn Yaeger
Jennifer Pooley
Laura Stein
Ruven Afanador
Jonathan Antin
Arthouse Management
Rich Aybar
Lawrence Aylward
Barbara Baum
Alisa Bentley
Beyoncé
Michael Birnbaum
Bono
Helaina Buzzeo
Elaine Canter
Jessica Carridi
Rosario Dawson
Mauro DiPreta
  and everyone
  at HarperEntertainment
Robert Downey Jr.
Paul Dupuy
John D'Urso
Alex Dymek
Nick Ellison
  and everyone at the
  Nicholas Ellison Agency
Molly Findlay
Magdalena Frackowiak
Nina Garcia
Jean Paul Gaultier
Greg the Bunny
Derek Jeter
Lynda Kahn
Faith Kates

William Lawrence
Hannah Lifson
Angela Lindvall
Carlos Lopez
Jennifer Love Hewitt
Todd MacIntire
David Marion
Ally Matteo
Carl and Terri Matteo
Gilles Mendel
Dan Milano
John Miserendino
Bibhu Mohapatra
Jessica Nagel
Caroline Noseworthy
Elena Paige
Mary-Louise Parker
Silvana Paternostro
Gunnar Petersen
Jane Puylagarde
Carine Roitfeld
Susan Romano
Michael Russo
Amanda Garcia Santana
Fiona Scarry
Richard Scarry
Jennifer Starr
Lisa Stevens
Trudie Styler
Charlotte Tilbury
Dita Von Teese
Christy Turlington
Gemma Ward
Daria Werbowy
Alex Wurtz
Robin Zendell